FARINELLI AND THE KING

Claire van Kampen

FARINELLI AND THE KING

OBERON BOOKS
LONDON

WWW.OBERONBOOKS.COM

First published in 2018 by Oberon Books Ltd
521 Caledonian Road, London N7 9RH
Tel: +44 (0) 20 7607 3637 / Fax: +44 (0) 20 7607 3629
e-mail: info@oberonbooks.com
www.oberonbooks.com

Reprinted with revisions in 2018 (twice)

A catalogue record for this book is available from the British Library.

PB ISBN: 9781786822949
E ISBN: 9781786822956

Cover photograph of Mark Rylance by Marc Brenner
Cover design by Spotco

Printed and bound by 4EDGE Limited, Hockley, Essex, UK.
eBook conversion by CPI Group (UK) Ltd, Croydon, CR0 4YY.

Farinelli and the King was originally commissioned by Dominic Dromgoole and produced by Shakespeare's Globe in 2015 for the Sam Wanamaker Playhouse, London. The production subsequently transferred to the Duke of York's Theatre in the West End of London, produced by Sonia Friedman Productions and Shakespeare's Globe, in association with Tulchin Bartner Productions and 1001 Nights.

The production opened on Broadway at the Belasco Theater in December 2017, produced by Sonia Friedman Productions, Shakespeare's Globe, Paula Marie Black, Tom Smedes, Peter Stern, Jane Bergère, Jane Dubin/Rachel Weinstein, 1001 Nights Productions, Elizabeth Cuthrell & Steven Tuttleman, Rupert Gavin, Robyn L. Paley, SGC USA, Tulchin Bartner Productions, Cindy & Jay Gutterman/Marc David Levine, Marguerite Hoffman/Van Kaplan and Shakespeare Road.

Playwright	Claire van Kampen
Director	John Dove
Designer	Jonathan Fensom
Lighting Designer	Paul Russell
UK Casting	Matilda James
US Casting	Jim Carnahan, C.S.A
Musical Arranger	Claire van Kampen
Music Supervisor	Bill Barclay
Hair and Wigs	Campbell Young Associates
Costume Coordinator	Lorraine Ebdon-Price
Voice and Dialect	Martin McKellan
Music Coordinator	David Titcomb
Assistant Music Arranger	Sophie Cotton

THE COMPANY

(Cast in order of appearance)

PHILIPPE V King of Spain / VINCENZO, a tailor in Bologna	Mark Rylance
MIGUEL, servant to the King / JETHRO, an opera house stagehand	Lucas Hall
ISABELLA FARNESE Queen of Spain	Melody Grove
DON SEBASTIAN DE LA CUADRA Chief Minister of Spain	Edward Peel
DR JOSÉ CERVI Physician to the King	Huss Garbiya
JOHN RICH Theatre Manager	Colin Hurley
FARINELLI (ACTOR) The famous castrato	Sam Crane
FARINELLI (SINGER)	Iestyn Davies James Hall Eric Jurenas
MUSICAL DIRECTOR / HARPSICHORD	Rob Howarth
ONSTAGE MUSICIANS	Pavlo Beznosiuk Chloe Fedor Kyle Miller Daniel Swenberg Jonathan Byers Pippa Macmillan
STAGE MANAGEMENT	Evangeline Rose Whitlock James Latus

ACT ONE

SCENE 1. MAY 1737.

The Palace. Madrid. Night.

The great ballroom, which is empty except for PHILIPPE, wearing a crown and a nightshirt and fishing from a goldfish bowl in the dark except for moonlight, which streams in through the casement window.

PHILIPPE speaking to the goldfish.

I see you are ignoring my bait; Kings shouldn't catch fish. Perhaps they fed you before, just to trick me into believing you're playing hard to catch. But I'm ahead of them all, you see. I know I am dreaming and they do not. Ah – you're thinking – how does he know he's dreaming, aren't you. Who would fish out of a goldfish bowl except in a dream! If I were mad, as they think I am, I would be fishing at noon when the sun's the very devil. Besides which, dreams happen by moonlight, everyone knows that, and the moon is full tonight. How blessed that at the outset of every such revolution you can remember nothing of the one before. How much happier you are, then, dear – I'm so sorry, I didn't quite catch your name… ALFONSO. Thank you. How much happier you are than I! Now to your other merits: *Leaning in intimately* I was touched by the confidence with which you speak to me of your affairs; and the cordiality of your offer to redress mine; the tender anxiety for my health – but I should tell you in the strictest confidence you understand…shh …here the body cares very little for the affairs of the mind;: at night you may be a favourite, and in the morning unknown.

Well…you won't be caught, that's a good omen. *(ISABELLA enters.)* Watch out! I nearly got him then.

ISABELLA: Philippe –

PHILIPPE: – Shh!

ISABELLA: What are you doing?

PHILIPPE: Isn't it obvious? Trying not to fish. *(He picks up the gold fish bowl, hugs it as if to protect it from her.)*

ISABELLA: Put the goldfish down.

PHILIPPE: I can't do that.

ISABELLA: Why not?

PHILIPPE: Might bite you.

ISABELLA: Goldfish don't bite.

PHILIPPE: This one's different.

ISABELLA: It's time you slept now.

PHILIPPE: I'll sleep when he sleeps.

ISABELLA: I don't think goldfish sleep.

PHILIPPE: How do you know?

ISABELLA: Come to bed.

PHILIPPE: Why have they brought my bed into the garden?

ISABELLA: If we were in the garden, the air would be cooler, and we would hear the nightbirds singing and the sound of crickets.

PHILIPPE: Nicely put. You can see can't you how they have succeeded in tricking you. You have stepped into my dream.

ISABELLA: Why is it a dream?

PHILIPPE: Do you really think I would be fishing from a goldfish bowl in my bedchamber?!

ISABELLA: Come with me. Leave that.

PHILIPPE: Why? Are you offering me sex?

ISABELLA: No…yes.

PHILIPPE: No, can't do. You are very beautiful tonight. But you don't understand – because you are not a King – that you are disturbing him, don't you see, just by being here in my dream. You must leave us in privacy if you please; he won't speak when you are near – and mind you take your beauty with you when you leave; it disturbs the moonlight. *(Looking up where the moon should be.)* Oh it's moved! And you're blocking my view of the stars tonight, which are very spectacular. *(To the goldfish.)* Don't you agree? The stars are wonderful tonight? Or do they look a little – distorted in your view? *(He gets down to goldfish level and tries to peer up through the water as if he were the fish.)* What? Oh yes. I do see what you mean.

ISABELLA: *(To the goldfish.)* There are no stars tonight; the moon is too bright for them.

PHILIPPE: *(To the fish.)* D'you hear that! 'the moon is too bright for them'!… Now what are we to do about that!… In a minute, I might go hunting.

ISABELLA: It's the middle of the night! You can't see to kill anything.

PHILIPPE: Why would I want to kill anything?!

ISABELLA: It's what you do on a hunt.

PHILIPPE: *(Laughs.)* Are you quite well?

He continues fishing

And another thing: I wouldn't be troubling the stable – men to saddle up any of those things they call horses. *(He points to painting of himself on his mare.)* All I have to do is climb into that painting and up on her back, and away we go… Simple isn't it. There, that one. Grizelda. Runs like the wind. Wonderful mare. Shame she's dead.

ISABELLA: If I sang to you, perhaps –

PHILIPPE: Oh don't do that! You have a voice like a frog!

His attention returns to the goldfish.

PHILIPPE: Look at the loyalty. He swims away and then returns to me over and over again.

ISABELLA picks up the goldfish bowl

PHILIPPE: Put it down. This is my dream, not yours. Stay out of it.

She puts the bowl down. Then goes over to the candles, which are mainly unlit. Starts to light them, one from another.

ISABELLA: – You need more light. Is it any wonder you think you are in the garden.

PHILIPPE: – *Che amore a nullo amar perdona* – 'Love allows nothing beloved to love another'… *(Notices the candles.)*

– Help! Fire! Help! I'll put it out! Run! Run!

He snatches the bowl from her and throws it and its contents at her –

Pause.

ISABELLA: Right… Right.

She leaves with dignity. He stands peacefully contemplating the fish which is flapping in a puddle of water. Picks the fish up and holds it in the palm of his hand.

My dear chap…come, let's get you by the fire. *(Moves to the candelabra and holds the fish to the light.)* Listen to me old chap: everything produced in this world has its shadow even at the beginning; when we are taken from the safety of the dark then are we no longer wholly ourselves; we have been claimed by others; it is how nations become great. Not all of us are equal; we were not born equal, we shall never be equal. You were born when the moon was increasing, and that's an end on it. *(The fish stops flapping. It is dead.)* Oh – oh! Well. Better off now. *Che amore a nullo amar perdona* – that is to say… 'Who love to nothing from loving' – or else it means 'who love to love nothing' and there again, it could be also…'loving comes to nothing'… but does it *actually* mean 'who love to nothing one from nothing,'…or…*sine qua non… in saecular saeculorum that is…* nothing nothing…nothing… Nothing……

(He lies down on the bed; places the fish on his forehead very carefully…) Love… See how it twists and falls…………

He closes his eyes. Then opens one.

Moon – if you're watching – I'm not asleep!

SCENE 2. THE PALACE, MADRID.

The King's bedchamber. Morning.

ISABELLA enters with DON SEBASTIAN DE LA CUADRA. She looks over to where PHILIPPE is asleep.

LA CUADRA: This cannot go on. Ma'am – I must report that the Council is unhappy.

ISABELLA: The King will not abdicate. I am sure of that.

LA CUADRA: But…you must see – his illness –

ISABELLA: –indisposition you mean? It will pass. If that's all?

Pause.

LA CUADRA: *(Picks up fish from PHILIPPE's forehead.)* Can you tell me about this*?*

ISABELLA: Oh. That. Yes. Last night. He became…agitated when I lit the candles.

LA CUADRA: His Majesty has become afraid of light?

ISABELLA: His Majesty is never afraid.

LA CUADRA: But…alarmed?

Pause.

ISABELLA: – the King has had an inflammation of the brain, that is all.

LA CUADRA: I can't contain this situation much longer – the council won't wear it! I'm telling you this as the King's chief minister –

ISABELLA: – Don Sebastian! As *our* chief minister, your *chieftest* duty, is to protect him, would you not agree?

LA CUADRA: – Ma'am I can no longer defend –

ISABELLA: – Look – the King –

PHILIPPE has stirred and wakes, sitting immediately upright and wide awake.

PHILIPPE: Is it time?

ISABELLA: It's ten in the morning. You've slept well. I'm glad.

PHILIPPE: I haven't slept a wink. What's the time *now* La Cuadra?

LA CUADRA: Er…

ISABELLA: Why, the same as before –

PHILIPPE: Useless! *(Exits.)*

ISABELLA: He was asleep. I came in during the night and saw.

LA CUADRA: How were you sure? He could have been pretending…

ISABELLA: He was whimpering in his sleep and talking very rapidly.

LA CUADRA: But this morning you hear how he thinks he has been awake. He doesn't know the difference. He –

PHILIPPE enters. He is covered in clocks of different weights and sizes and ages.

PHILIPPE: You see how time lies? Look at this one – ten o'clock. But this – five past ten. This one nine – thirty-five. Look? *(He shoves the clock face towards them.)* Do you see?

LA CUADRA: Yes indeed.

PHILIPPE: Here's a riddle for you La Cuadra. What have you and these clocks got in common?

LA CUADRA: I can't imagine.

PHILIPPE: They're showing me different faces, and I can't tell which one is true. *(Pause while he examines the effect on LA CUADRA.)* Where do I live? In the past present or future? Who can tell me?

LA CUADRA: Your Majesty –

PHILIPPE: You can't. Yet it's so simple. But you're not, are you La Cuadra.

ISABELLA: Don Sebastian is concerned for you, Philippe.

PHILIPPE: God is concerned for me. And for you too, Isabella. But perhaps not for him. *(Looking at LA CUADRA.)* Although God loves a sinner.

LA CUADRA: Your Majesty means– ?

PHILIPPE: Pretending you don't know? Oh – Isabella can you take these to bed please? They've been working hard all night. They are running down. Look. Quite run-down. Well done, well done! Some of you have done better than others but I love you all the same, you know. Despite your faults. *(He starts to pile them on LA CUADRA.)* I love you too, La Cuadra, despite *your* faults. God loves us all. Even you. Amazing, isn't it. Take them to their rest. Good night sweet sinners, good night!

ISABELLA: Philippe. Don Sebastian has come to help you.

PHILIPPE: Help me? Ha!

LA CUADRA: Your Majesty, please, it's time; the council –

PHILIPPE: the Council are a pack of wolves–Stay away, Isabella! They bite!

LA CUADRA: *(To ISABELLA.)* This has gone far enough.

ISABELLA: *(To LA CUADRA)* Don't, just let me, – he'll listen – *(She holds out her hand. He doesn't move.)*

PHILIPPE: (*Overlapping ISABELLA.*)Where is far enough? You want to get rid of me. That's it, La Cuadra. Isn't it.

ISABELLA looks helplessly at LA CUADRA.

PHILIPPE: What's been going on?

He looks from one to another. Suddenly his mood has changed.

PHILIPPE: What have you been plotting while I've been asleep?

ISABELLA: I don't know what you mean! *(Looks at LA CUADRA.)*

PHILIPPE: What was that?

ISABELLA: What was what?

PHILIPPE: That look.

ISABELLA: We didn't –

PHILIPPE: – you are going to get rid of me.

ISABELLA: No, no, of course not, why would we –

PHILIPPE: You think I am mad.

ISABELLA: No.

PHILIPPE: – you want me clapped up so you can run my kingdom without me!

ISABELLA: No!

LA CUADRA: Your majesty, calm yourself.

PHILIPPE: Time. It's time. You said. We've all lost time. You're trying to make me lose my mind. Between their time and mine, But I won't. I won't. I'm holding on to it and you can't take this head from here and put it here… *(Gestures to the clocks.)* – All those poor creatures… Can you hear the ticking?! *(To LA CUADRA.)* Get out! Get out before I lose my mind!

LA CUADRA: Sire –

PHILIPPE: – Now!

LA CUADRA exits (to get DR CERVI).

ISABELLA: Philippe.

PHILIPPE: I have to get these away from you. You're dangerous. *(Starts to pull the chaise longue.)*

ISABELLA: Philippe, I –

PHILIPPE: You are getting rid of me. Of us all.

ISABELLA: No one is going to get rid of you, they're just concerned –

PHILIPPE: – about –

ISABELLA: – last night. I thought –

PHILIPPE: – you think too much! That's dangerous here in Madrid! –

ISABELLA: – yes, yes, you are right –

PHILIPPE: – and if you are dangerous then I cannot have you near my children – I will have them withdrawn into the country.

ISABELLA: – the children? But I am their mother!

PHILIPPE: Not of my real children. Only six others. Bastards.

ISABELLA: What?! You – *you* are their father.

PHILIPPE: I have seen you. At night. Stealing out secretly.

ISABELLA: When?!

PHILIPPE: When you think I am asleep, I watch you. I have seen you sliding along in the dark to meet –

ISABELLA: – this is ridiculous!

PHILIPPE: Do you deny your children have been fathered by Don Diego Gomez Los Cobos y luna of 49 Pareda Street, Madrid, on the morning of the…

ISABELLA: *(Laughs.)* Yes I do deny it!

PHILIPPE: Liar! You would have Don Diego's offspring run my Kingdom, would you?

ISABELLA: No! No…*you*, you are their father…and my King, a *good* King who –

PHILIPPE: Liar!

PHILIPPE attacks her, knocking her off balance.

ISABELLA stays very quiet

PHILIPPE: Oh *now* you have nothing to say. Mutinous, eh?

ISABELLA: I pray for your better health, your majesty.

He hits her so hard she is knocked to the floor.

She lies face down, but we see she is conscious and very aware of what to do next. She stays very still.

PHILIPPE: Who *are* you? Who *are* you?

LA CUADRA, who has heard all behind the door, rushes in with the King's doctor JOSE CERVI in tow.

PHILIPPE: *(Runs away, throwing his dressing gown at them.)* Quick! Blow out the lights! *(Hides behind the drapes.)*

LA CUADRA: Quickly Dr Cervi, before he can hurt Her Majesty again.

PHILIPPE: *(Whispers.)* Liars! Liars! They would take my life with their lying!

Truly, this is a dreadful punishment, to be alone in this fearful country at the end of the world! – the hot sun that makes my head split…too much light – I lack for what I need. There is nothing here… Nothing of what I know.

LA CUADRA: Give him a draught Dr Cervi.

DR CERVI gently pulls aside the drapes to reveal PHILIPPE; holds out his hand to PHILIPPE, who takes it, as if he was a child.

PHILIPPE: Doctor Cervi. *(Aside.)* I am not afraid of him. We are perfectly in control Isabella. *(Looks over at her, but she stays motionless.)*

LA CUADRA: Take him back to his bedchamber, Dr Cervi, and sedate him while I attend to her Majesty.

CERVI: Leave it to me.

CERVI leads PHILIPPE from the room.

PHILIPPE is now entirely passive, like a child.

PHILIPPE: Thank you. Most kind. Thank you. *(Exits with DR CERVI.)*

ISABELLA: I am unhurt.

LA CUADRA: Madam.

ISABELLA: Please do not fuss about me.

LA CUADRA: I cannot let this happen again.

ISABELLA: It was not the King's fault.

LA CUADRA: His Majesty is now so unstable I fear for your safety.

ISABELLA: I did provoke him.

LA CUADRA: Ma'am I saw it all and you did not.

ISABELLA: What do you suggest I do?

LA CUADRA: Leave the palace immediately.

ISABELLA: Leave?

LA CUADRA: Until we can restore the King to a calmer state.

ISABELLA: How long will that be?

LA CUADRA: Once calm is established I can allow you to return to Madrid.

ISABELLA: This is so cruel!

LA CUADRA: It is a cruel illness Madam.

ISABELLA: What shall you do with him?

LA CUADRA: There are methods which other Christian doctors are keen to try.

ISABELLA: Oh God. Oh God, what will they do to him.

LA CUADRA: You must leave that to them.

ISABELLA: But they would –

LA CUADRA: You must go home.

ISABELLA: Italy? No, my home is here. Everything I am, everything I love is here. Senor La Cuadra, I cannot, will not go. *(Exit followed by LA CUADRA.)*

SCENE 3. LONDON, 11 JUNE 1737.

Backstage at the opera, in Lincoln's Inn Fields, during the interval of an opera. The frontcloth is coming in – we see the back of it.

The sound of an orchestra tuning; stagehands calling to each other from the other side of the cloth. Properties removed from the stage are brought backstage. The theatre impresario JOHN RICH enters with JETHRO, his assistant.

JETHRO: *(Calling to a stagehand offstage.)* Bring in the flies! Bring it in! *(To JOHN RICH.)* It's chaos outside guv'. They're shouting 'Farinelli! Farinelli!' all the way down the Strand!

RICH: Get rid of them! It's only the interval! And keep them away from the stage door. And get him out before the last curtain call.

JETHRO: *(Exiting.)* Cut the last call?

RICH: *(Calls after him.)* No, I'll do the last call. Give them my jig. They like a nice Jig. *(Stagehands come on and off giving him bouquets for FARINELLI so that he's drowning in flowers.)* It'll take the edge off… *(A stagehand says something offstage he can't hear: 'the queen is coming round'.)* What? *(Stagehand: 'queen', RICH still can't hear.)* Who? *(He sits down on a piece of property.)* Just when you're trying to get a bit of peace, think about what you'd like for dinner; half a dozen oysters…a chop; some nice port… *(JETHRO brings him a bill.)* Yes I know – four pounds ten for smelling salts! Why can't these bloody women learn not to faint! *(Looking at the cards on the flowers.)* Farinelli, Farinelli, Farinelli, Farinelli…all for him and none for me. *(To JETHRO.)* What do I have to do? Stand upside down in a bucket of custard and quote Shakespeare? Too many bloody theatres to run. That's my problem. *(ISABELLA, who is dressed for the opera, appears upstage unseen by RICH and JETHRO having walked around the cloth.)* Priscilla said as much and she was right; damn woman. Why did I ever marry her! She's been on my case since we opened – 'It's not as good as the Beggar's Opera, John; why don't you put that on again, John… These Aye-talian singers…men singing like girls…they're not normal'… Not normal! I could kill her. But she's right. They're not. *(RICH notices ISABELLA.)*

ISABELLA: How can you bear it! His voice!

RICH: You've lost your way. This –

ISABELLA: – I am shaking! *(Holds out her hands.)* You see – still shaking!

RICH: This is backstage.

ISABELLA: I am almost in a fever – my heart is still beating so fast – his singing –

RICH: Farinelli won't see you; he never sees anyone in the interval. Not even me. Jethro will show you out – *(Stagehand drops something offstage and it smashes; RICH puts his head in his hands as JETHRO exits. Under his breath:)* Irreplaceable.

ISABELLA: – The music! What an opera! Have you seen it?

RICH: I produced it. *(JETHRO brings him a glass of pie and port and exits.)* As you can see, Madame, the interval is a busy time for us.

ISABELLA: When he appeared onstage, I was not impressed; nor by the sudden standing ovation he received; I thought that vulgar. Then…he began. A long note, held; I must think it was beyond a minute. A swooping, soaring sound and the notes were above the tree-tops, bird-like, unimaginable. When the aria finished just now I couldn't help my tears; I was unable to move; I just stared at the stage, where he had been…I couldn't believe what I had seen and heard… I felt something had profoundly changed within me. … and then, – I knew…

RICH: You knew? What?

ISABELLA: That I must hope somehow to bring Farinelli to Spain with me.

JETHRO enters with the leader of the orchestra holding his violin.

RICH: NO! The answer is NO. Pay rises are out. If you'd all care to play in tune I'll think about it. *(Disgruntled band leader and JETHRO go off – JOHN RICH calls after.)* – and only three encores! – I'm not paying for four! And not too fast with my jig; not with my lungs…bastards…Please excuse me, Madame; at the end of the evening I shall be only too delighted to help – but we can't hold the curtain, there's Royalty present!

ISABELLA: My business with you is simply this; I must return to Spain immediately, and I need Farinelli to accompany me.

RICH: What?!

ISABELLA: His audience in Spain would be very…special.

RICH: We can talk about this after the performance – and so – *(Steers her towards the exit in the wings.)*

ISABELLA: I have no time to wait. I must have my answer now.

RICH: I cannot answer for the Maestro.

ISABELLA: I have heard differently, Mr. Rich.

RICH: Then I have to say no on his behalf.

ISABELLA: He must cherish your care of him.

RICH: Yes. Yes he does. So many people want a piece of him. Look, I understand how you are feeling, Madame, how the music has moved you. *(Looks at his time-piece.)* Goodness me! One minute before Act Four! *(Calls.)* Jethro!

ISABELLA: Isn't it wonderful here, backstage! So many people doing things with ropes – I have heard it said here in London that your theatre is…how can I put it…struggling to survive. That must make life difficult for you.

RICH: Madam…we are artists…we manage.

ISABELLA: – Yes, artists always do don't they. But Farinelli is expensive… *(Handing him a purse full of gold.)* He need not know of this.

RICH: *(Does not look at the purse.)* Madam…you are too generous –

ISABELLA: Think of it as a contribution.

RICH: – but I cannot –

ISABELLA: The world is full of wonderful singers, Mr Rich. For the price of one Farinelli –

RICH: – No –

ISABELLA: – A whole stable-full.

RICH: No.

ISABELLA: Think of your rivals.

ISABELLA hands RICH the purse. He doesn't take it. Looks at it.

She makes a small ceremony of handing him the purse and placing it in his hand.

RICH: Madam I regret – *(He hands the purse back to her but she refuses it.)*

ISABELLA: I ask you again: if you let Farinelli travel with me tonight –

RICH: – Madam –

ISABELLA: – I will recompense your purse for a whole Season.

RICH: Madam, you flatter me beyond all words. *(He hands the purse back to her, places it in her hand, bows.)*

ISABELLA: Ah. What a pity. This theatre would have been the finest in London with me as your patron.

The sound of an orchestra tuning up

RICH: – oh what a shame, the interval is over, our interview must be concluded *(He clicks his fingers.)* Jethro! *(And JETHRO appears.)* Mrs. is leaving, please escort her back to her seat –

ISABELLA: If you change your mind… Here is my address… *(She hands him a note; he looks at it. Realises. With horror.)*

RICH: Oh. *(Realizes he should be bowing, tries to do so…)*

ISABELLA: I must take my leave of you, Sir… Guard your… bird well. And do tell him how his song inspired me. *(Exits, followed by JETHRO.)*

RICH: Majesty, I will.

He looks after her. It is strongly in his mind to speak again, but she is gone.

RICH: Shit.

SCENE 4. THE PALACE, MADRID.

Mid June. A receiving room. Early evening.

DR CERVI enters followed by LA CUADRA.

LA CUADRA: Why is she coming back so soon? Did you know?

CERVI: Of course not.

LA CUADRA: She will want to see the King, and we're not ready.

CERVI: How do we tell her?

LA CUADRA: She'll find out soon enough. If only she'd given me more time –

Headstrong woman! Over-educated.

CERVI: – Well – but she –

LA CUADRA: Ungovernable. She's had her own way from the day she set foot in Spain–sacking people left right and centre –

ISABELLA enters, she has just set foot in the Palace.

Dear Majesty! *(He bows low.)* How happy is Spain to see you back!

ISABELLA: You are Spain are you now, Sir? I have been away too long it seems…

LA CUADRA: Ma'am –

ISABELLA: – I trust that you are well?

LA CUADRA: Quite well Majesty. However –

ISABELLA: And the King?

LA CUADRA: When you left for London Ma'am we were very afraid.

ISABELLA: I blame myself for leaving him. Did he ask for me?

LA CUADRA: Ma'am, he did not. At times he would burst into uncontrollable weeping, saying that grief had entered him. He wishes to die. And now –

ISABELLA: Yes?

LA CUADRA: He has fallen into some kind of sleeping state that is not sleeping.

CERVI: We don't yet understand it.

ISABELLA: Have you bled him?

LA CUADRA: Dr. Cervi doesn't believe in it.

ISABELLA: Let me see him alone.

LA CUADRA: No Madam. You must not. It's not wise.

ISABELLA: *(To the servants.)* Bring him here, to this chamber. We will set him down just here.

LA CUADRA: No, I urge you, he –

ISABELLA: I have a present for him I would like to wake him to receive.

LA CUADRA: If you disturb him – we do not know enough – it could be very dangerous –

ISABELLA: I will be the judge of that. Please do as I say. *(She exits very quickly.)*

LA CUADRA looks at CERVI.

LA CUADRA: Doctor Cervi, you and I know what must happen now.

CERVI: You'll inform the Council?

LA CUADRA: Yes, and stand the King's successor by. This is the procedure: I will bring the King official documents which you and I both know he will be unable to read or sign; I will then pass you the abdication papers for your signature as Doctor in attendance. The Queen will witness.

CERVI: Then his reign will be over!

LA CUADRA: There's nothing left to try.

LA CUADRA exits as ISABELLA enters again.

PHILIPPE, seemingly fast asleep but with his eyes wide open registering nothing, is carried into the chamber by servants, and set down on the chaise longue. ISABELLA sees the sleeping king and is delighted, apprehensive. She goes over to one of the other chamber doors, opens one slightly, looks at PHILIPPE, still asleep.

There is a silence. She nods at the footman who in turn nods to another in the antechamber, who signals:

Music: FARINELLI's voice offstage sings 'Ho Perso' from 'Il Parnasso in Festa' by Handel (first few bars of recit only to the first cadence) with offstage musicians. The sound is extraordinary. Unearthly. At the end of the aria, PHILIPPE stirs, blinks his eyes.

PHILIPPE: Something woke me. Was it you, singing? I heard singing.

ISABELLA: You know I can't sing.

PHILIPPE: Perhaps I am not awake.

ISABELLA: Yes, yes at last you are. You have come back to me.

PHILIPPE: You are so beautiful that I must still be asleep.

ISABELLA: I am here; you are awake.

He looks at her.

PHILIPPE: I have woken from a dream of you, to you. Is it you? *(Smells her.)* You seem like you.

ISABELLA: It is me.

PHILIPPE: Do you know how much I love you? Only you. I have missed you; think of that, what it is to be missed.

ISABELLA: Dear one, I am back now and I shall stay by your side.

PHILIPPE: Oh. *(Beat.)* I am frightened that now you are back; it will all come back; the thoughts, all come back. I must sleep again.

ISABELLA: Don't you want to hear more singing before you decide that?

PHILIPPE: Is there more?

She pushes at the door that has been ajar; it has been a pre-arranged signal; FARINELLI enters. He is dressed in a highly decorated manner, with great taste and elegance. Though not dressed as a King, ie with a crown etc, the effect is also strangely regal.

PHILIPPE: Who's that?

ISABELLA: It is Maestro Farinelli; you know – the greatest singer in the world, and come to sing for you.

PHILIPPE: He looks like a king.

FARINELLI: No your Majesty, I am not.

PHILIPPE: Don't call me your majesty.

ISABELLA: Philippe!

PHILIPPE: Well it's a fraud.

FARINELLI: What would you have me sing?

PHILIPPE: Ah. How delightful! Instead of pondering the question of whether we should invade this country or that, we simply decide what to have you sing!

ISABELLA: Maestro Far –

FARINELLI: Carlo, please.

ISABELLA: The Maestro can sing many arias to delight you.

PHILIPPE: How dreadful!

ISABELLA: Farinelli can sing in your own language, or mine.

PHILIPPE: He can, can he? Then let's have a language neither of us are equally familiar with.

ISABELLA: Oh. Singing is so beautiful in Italian.

PHILIPPE: *(To FARINELLI.)* Do you agree with that, Maestro not-a-king-thingy-nelli?

FARINELLI: I have recently enjoyed singing in English.

PHILIPPE: Aha! A philistine! Wonderful! Let's have some English then!

ISABELLA: Herr Handel lives in England but writes in Italian, because Italian is –

PHILIPPE: – the language of fools. I am not eager for *you* to stay. I wish you to leave us.

ISABELLA: Oh! *(She is very disappointed.)* If you say so, of course.

PHILIPPE: I do say so. *(ISABELLA curtsies.)*

ISABELLA: Your Majesty. *(She goes to leave.)*

PHILIPPE: Doctor Cervi.

CERVI exits.

PHILIPPE: It was you singing out there, wasn't it.

FARINELLI: Yes.

PHILIPPE: You interrupted my dream.

FARINELLI: I'm sorry if I did.

PHILIPPE: It's good you're sorry. Why were you singing?

FARINELLI: I wanted to.

Beat.

PHILIPPE: What were you singing about?

FARINELLI: Love. Loss.

PHILIPPE: Is that about goldfish?

FARINELLI: No.

PHILIPPE: Are you sure?

FARINELLI: Yes.

Beat.

PHILIPPE: Here's a fine game. I ask you questions. If you answer correctly you don't get your head cut off.

FARINELLI: I'm no good at games. I always lose.

PHILIPPE: Oh I'll give you a tip. Tell the truth! There, that's easy isn't it?

FARINELLI: It should be.

PHILIPPE: Should be. Hmm.

Pause.

FARINELLI: Just one thing about this game.

PHILIPPE: Yes? What's that?

FARINELLI: I am supposing that you are asking me questions to which you already know the right answers.

PHILIPPE: Why do you suppose that?

FARINELLI: because if you didn't already know the answers to the questions you are about to ask me, how would you know if I am telling you the truth?

PHILIPPE: Oh very good! Got a point. Could be a problem.

FARINELLI: Seeing as you know nothing about me.

PHILIPPE: *(Thinks.)* But I do have a solution to that.

FARINELLI: You do?

PHILIPPE: Yes. But I can't tell you what it is.

FARINELLI: You can't?

PHILIPPE: No.

FARINELLI: Why?

PHILIPPE: I can't tell you that either. Sorry to be a bit tricky about it.

FARINELLI: That's quite all right.

PHILIPPE: Good! We have a perfect understanding! So here we go…

FARINELLI: So these are the questions, now?

PHILIPPE: Yes! Number one: where were you born?

FARINELLI: Andria. In Italy.

PHILIPPE: *(Saying it a split second after FARINELLI.)* – Andria, in Italy. I knew it! Number two… What was two… How old are you?

FARINELLI: Thirty-two.

PHILIPPE: Show me your teeth.

FARINELLI opens his mouth. PHILIPPE takes a good look inside.

PHILIPPE: You do have thirty-two teeth, it's true…but they're…

FARINELLI: I like sweet things. Sugar.

PHILIPPE: Oh you should get on top of that. Nutrition, nutrition, nutrition.

Question number – four –

FARINELLI: – three.

PHILIPPE: – four: Who taught you to sing?

FARINELLI: Porpora.

PHILIPPE: Like him? Good teacher?

FARINELLI: No, and yes. Yes.

PHILIPPE: Trained up lots like you?

FARINELLI: A few.

Beat.

PHILIPPE: Your voice. It's not natural, is it.

FARINELLI: No.

PHILIPPE: Neither is it natural, that I am a king. Do you know that?

FARINELLI: No.

PHILIPPE: Do you dream?

FARINELLI: No. Or at least, I forget them before I wake up.

PHILIPPE: We all dream. Most of us would prefer to forget our dreams. Perhaps you need to forget yours. When were you made King?

FARINELLI: I am not a king.

PHILIPPE: I am afraid you are. We were both made kings against our will. You have a world of subjects – as I do. Mine were given to me by God, though. I wish I were a pagan.

FARINELLI: Why?

PHILIPPE: Many gods are fun; one is a nightmare. Being King isn't normal. So He keeps us on a tight rein. When were *you* robbed of your normality?

FARINELLI: I was ten years old.

Pause.

PHILIPPE: When they did that to you? That is too old and also too young for such brutality.

FARINELLI: Yes. *(It is painful for him to talk about.)*

PHILIPPE: Who did it?

FARINELLI: My brother. How were you made a King?

PHILIPPE: My grandfather ordered it. Louis the Sun King. I loved him. I still do. I was his favourite grandson. I was seventeen. But I am not Spanish. I am an imposter.

FARINELLI: I loved my brother.

PHILIPPE: Why did he do this to you?

FARINELLI: For money. It was illegal of course; they blamed it on a fall from a horse. He wrote beautiful music for me though.

PHILIPPE: An angel with a knife in his hand made Farinelli.

ISABELLA enters.

FARINELLI: Yes. Would you have me sing now?

ISABELLA: I do think that Maestro Farinelli should begin.

PHILIPPE: How do I know it's really him? Question number five: are you famous?

FARINELLI: No. Farinelli is famous.

PHILIPPE: Hah! Very good. Extremely?

FARINELLI: Extremely.

PHILIPPE: She *(looking at ISABELLA)* collects famous things. *(Confidentially.)* Because she's Italian.

ISABELLA: Really I think my dear that –

PHILIPPE: Here's another question. How long can you hold a note for?

FARINELLI: Two and a half minutes.

ISABELLA is concerned and exasperated. It's not going to plan.

ISABELLA: His range is nearly three octaves. Even amongst other castrati his voice is considered unique –

PHILIPPE: 'Even amongst other castrati' – a vile phrase. That's a vile phrase. Leave us.

ISABELLA: *(Slightly at a loss.)* You should hear him sing… *(Exits.)*

PHILIPPE: Do you think I don 't know why you've come here, Maestro Farinelli? To visit this aberration of a King in his boghole of a wilderness where there is no *music*, only the brutish clapping of swarthy dancers in the streets and the foul strumming of Spanish guitars! Indeed! For you, *you* to come here with the pretense of charming this fake king from his dearest wish, (which is to simply to die) with melodious airs and your very sweet-toothed disposition – well! You can understand that this beggars belief.

FARINELLI: Her majesty – asked me to come.

PHILIPPE: My wife! You were to sing Handel! People had paid to see you! Where's your sense of civic responsibility?

FARINELLI: She said you needed me.

PHILIPPE: I might have to cut your head off.

FARINELLI: I hope I get to sing first.

Pause.

PHILIPPE: I am not wanted here. Do you know that?

FARINELLI: No.

PHILIPPE: I am not loved here. If you stay, you will not be loved too.

Beat.

Doesn't that alarm you?

FARINELLI: No.

PHILIPPE: Well, well. You have correctly answered all my questions save one.

FARINELLI: And what is that?

PHILIPPE: Why you are here.

FARINELLI: I have answered that.

PHILIPPE: You were sent to report upon me? To them?

FARINELLI: Them?

PHILIPPE: Don't play with me. Remember. *(He pantomimes his head being severed from his neck and the head bouncing down on to the floor and along it.)*

FARINELLI: I'm a singer. I can never remember what people have told me. Names. Jokes, anecdotes. Unless they have been set to music.

PHILIPPE: Like a bird then. Bird-brained.

FARINELLI: Exactly like a bird.

PHILIPPE: Sing to me now.

FARINELLI: *(Looks around, there are no musicians in sight.)* I'll sing a capella then?

PHILIPPE: A capella, Acapulco, upside down, arse about tit, whatever you like, as long as you sing, it matters not to me. Isabella! *(ISABELLA enters very quickly; she has been listening outside the door.)* I am convinced he is who he says he is. I don't need to see his balls. Or the lack of them. He's going to sing for us. Well don't just stand there! Find someone to fetch his music.

ISABELLA: But I – oh! – *(Exits exasperated. Offstage:)* For God's sake!

PHILIPPE: Ten years old you say.

FARINELLI: Yes.

PHILIPPE: So painful. Poor child. Can you fuck women?

FARINELLI: Yes, if I want to.

PHILIPPE: Do you want to?

ISABELLA enters

PHILIPPE: My darling! He can fuck women!

This isn't the statement ISABELLA was expecting. She looks bewildered.

ISABELLA: I am sorry, Maestro. You can see that the king –

PHILIPPE: That's extraordinary! To sing like that and also to be able to fuck!

ISABELLA: I came to say –

PHILIPPE: – she came to say –

ISABELLA: That the musicians are ready.

PHILIPPE: Ah, 'the readiness is all'. I feel my passion come upon me. *(To ISABELLA.)* You must stop and he must sing! Give her a kiss Farinelli!

FARINELLI does not.

ISABELLA: The musicians are waiting. When you are ready, Maestro.

PHILIPPE: – Good. We will make music now, together. We will keep out that world and have only this. *(He claps his hands.)*

FARINELLI starts singing 'Alto Giove' from 'Polifemo' by Porpora (A section only) without waiting for the introduction, perfectly on the pitch. He continues. The music joins… Near the end, CERVI enters… When it is finished… It is a very pregnant moment.

It's a long time since I felt I wanted something, anything. Oh – I have something for you! *(He takes up a gold coronet, blowing the dust off it.)* Let us exchange clothing.

FARINELLI: But you have only a nightshirt.

PHILIPPE: Well, you give me your clothes. We are the same size. *(FARINELLI takes off his jacket and gives it to PHILIPPE, who dresses in it.)*

Oh this is good, don't you agree? Now I am a King again, I feel it! And you must have this… *(Places the coronet on his head.)* …and you are crowned, and now we are equal! Inside and out!

FARINELLI: Not quite, I think.

PHILIPPE: No… I do not have your voice, that is certain…ten years old…ten…

LA CUADRA enters carrying a sheaf of papers.

LA CUADRA: Majesty. The council is convened. I have here the defense budget and projection of military expenditure for the fiscal year 1738 – and you know, this must be signed off immediately. *(LA CUADRA gives PHILIPPE the papers and looks knowingly at DR CERVI. PHILIPPE glances at the document for a few seconds, then – his attention seems to be elsewhere…)*

LA CUADRA: *(Looks meaningfully at DR CERVI…as if to say 'get ready'.)* Your Majesty, I must ask you to please sign the budget for me.

PHILIPPE is not looking at the document, but waving it over a candle as if to unconsciously burn it.

ISABELLA: Philippe!

PHILIPPE's head lolls backwards and he shuts his eyes; the document, seemingly forgotten, is held close to the candle flames; he is now muttering under his breath…deep in thought.

LA CUADRA: *(To ISABELLA.)* Your Majesty…you see that I have no option. Dr Cervi, would you now sign the King's abdication papers?

ISABELLA: No!

LA CUADRA hands DR CERVI the papers to sign. ISABELLA looks on in anguish.

FARINELLI: *(To PHILIPPE.)* Your Majesty. *(PHILIPPE immediately 'returns'.)*

PHILIPPE: *(Suddenly attending to the document.)* You've made a mistake in paragraph two, haven't you, La Cuadra? Look – see there? That's not right. You've omitted the revenue from the Basque regions – that's careless of you, because they generally pay up on time…and that would mean… twenty more cannons, five hundred muskets and one ton of shot, wouldn't it.

LA CUADRA: Yes…I see…

PHILIPPE: – and is that all we are pulling from the asiento contract? Tut tut! Things are slipping I see, we need more impetus; what's our ambassador doing? Isn't that what he's there for? Seriously, La Cuadra, you need to get a grip – your predecessor would never have let this slide – I'm going to the Council.

LA CUADRA: Your Majesty, I –

ISABELLA: (*Giving a triumphant look.)* I will accompany his Majesty. We will go together.

LA CUADRA: *(At a total loss to understand.)* But perhaps his Majesty would like to prepare, first? *(Looks askance at the King's clothing.)*

ISABELLA: Not necessary. His Majesty is quite prepared.

LA CUADRA: I meant, merely, Ma'am that his Majesty may care to don something more…suitable.

PHILIPPE: Oh this is quite suitable!

ISABELLA: Maestro Farinelli, I bid you make yourself as comfortable as you wish. Everything here is for your enjoyment.

PHILIPPE: Except the food. You won't like it. Spanish, they won't cook anything else.

FARINELLI: I am at your disposition, Ma'am.

PHILIPPE is suddenly in two minds.

PHILIPPE: And mine?

FARINELLI: Of course.

PHILIPPE: I want to stay with Farinelli. To hear more.

ISABELLA: *(To PHILIPPE, holds out her arm.)* Shall we go?

PHILIPPE: Why?

ISABELLA: It will please them.

PHILIPPE: I care not for pleasing them.

ISABELLA: Then it would please me.

PHILIPPE: For you, my love. *(He takes her arm.)*

Now Don Sebastian, we are going to the Council. I'm sorry, La Cuadra, that life seems so difficult for you. What is my bed doing here? Please ensure that Maestro Farinelli has all to his comfort in his apartments.

LA CUADRA is furious that he is being commanded thus, but bows.

PHILIPPE: I'd like to remind you, La Cuadra, that it was I, a Frenchman, who reformed the entire tax system of this country. Olé!

LA CUADRA: Indeed, Sire.

PHILIPPE: You've got a lot to be grateful for.

LA CUADRA: Majesty. As ever.

ISABELLA: We leave the Maestro in your care.

PHILIPPE: So don't fuck it up.

LA CUADRA bows. He is both furious and confused.

PHILIPPE and ISABELLA leave the chamber. DR CERVI follows them. LA CUADRA and FARINELLI are therefore on their own.

LA CUADRA: Signor Farinelli –

FARINELLI: Senor La Cuadra.

LA CUADRA: Like London, did you?

FARINELLI: Yes. Though the weather's terrible.

LA CUADRA: Drink a lot of tea there?

FARINELLI: I never touch it.

LA CUADRA: Make a lot of friends there? Important people?

Awkward pause.

FARINELLI: Senor. I have come to sing for his Majesty, that is all. I think I can help him.

LA CUADRA: Signor Farinelli – permit me – a word of advice… the King cannot be cured by a song. He cannot be cured at all. Let me not detain you further. I will of course see that your clothes are returned to you.

FARINELLI: Oh, they belong to the King now. Please do not him disturb him on my account.

LA CUADRA: I will make sure they are pressed. For your journey home. Good day, Signor.

Exits. LA CUADRA stays low in an extended over-formal bow until FARINELLI has left

DR CERVI enters, on the heels of FARINELLI's exit

LA CUADRA: Did you know about this?

CERVI: Farinelli? No; the Queen wanted to surprise us.

LA CUADRA: *(Exasperated.)* Tut!

CERVI: He seems genuinely keen to help –

LA CUADRA: Help whom?

CERVI: – but you've seen for yourself – the King –

LA CUADRA: I've seen nothing new. The King's illness is a straightforward case of Possession.

CERVI: I don't agree.

LA CUADRA: Dr Juevo, Dr Armandino – far more eminent doctors than you – agree with me: when the Devil's in town – drive him out! That's what they say. I see no reason to disagree with that. Do you?

CERVI: – Theirs may be the traditional view, –

LA CUADRA: – It's God's view, Dr Cervi. Would you argue with Him?

CERVI: As the King's Doctor, I am of the opinion that the King's illness has turned.

LA CUADRA: Then, Doctor, it is a miracle, and we have Dr Juevo's prayers to thank for it.

CERVI: No, we have Farinelli to thank for it.

LA CUADRA: – Oh? and what do I say to the Church? 'Put away the Bibles, we've got bits of opera instead?' Doctor Cervi, be reasonable!

CERVI: Isn't Farinelli's voice also part of God's plan?

LA CUADRA: *(Beat.)* You have a week. One. Until the feast of Sant Joan. Then I'll be booting this Fancy Nellie back to England where he belongs.

LA CUADRA exits, furious, passed by ISABELLA as she enters.

SCENE 5. CONTINUOUS.

ISABELLA: To hear the King laugh! I had forgotten the sound. How can a human voice change a man's life?

CERVI: We don't yet know…

ISABELLA: But in time – we'll find out more and then –

CERVI: – Farinelli is under contract in London, is he not?

ISABELLA: But now he is with us, and that is all that matters now! *(FARINELLI enters.)* Oh – Maestro! *(CERVI bows and exits, very thoughtful.)* You are like Orpheus – you know, in the old tale!

FARINELLI: Orpheus? Why?

ISABELLA: Taming the wild beasts with his singing! It would make a great opera! Perhaps you will sing it one day.

FARINELLI: Perhaps. *(Beat.)* Although…

ISABELLA: Yes?

FARINELLI: When I sang to him…something was so different.

ISABELLA: How?

FARINELLI: It is in the way he listens; it's as if he is leaning in to hear it more particularly.

ISABELLA: That must please you.

FARINELLI: It does. It's not what I had expected.

ISABELLA: You have given us hope, Maestro.

FARINELLI: Hope is a very great responsibility.

PHILIPPE enters. He is still dressed mainly in the habit he left in, and is carrying a book of sheet music, followed by MIGUEL, who is bearing many music books.

PHILIPPE: Farinelli – here you are!

ISABELLA: Philippe – what's all that?

PHILIPPE: Music! All we can find! Miguel – show him!

FARINELLI looks through the music books with MIGUEL.

ISABELLA: But how was the Council?

PHILIPPE: Older.

ISABELLA: What were they discussing?

PHILIPPE: War. I left. They'll have me kill but they won't give me a knife to eat my dinner…

ISABELLA: You have forgotten. Last Christmas, you stabbed poor Miguel in the leg when he was serving you.

PHILIPPE: What?!! When??!! Miguel? *(He turns to look at the servant behind him.)* Dear Miguel!! Why? Why would I do such a thing? *(He is thrown by this realization, and all the energy seems to drain from him; he stands, slumped; drifts. The music book falls to the floor.)*

ISABELLA: Miguel. Get Doctor Cervi. *(MIGUEL exits.)*

FARINELLI: Let me help you.

Together they help PHILIPPE to a chair. He sits, lifelessly. ISABELLA looks concerned – she expected PHILIPPE to stay well…

PHILIPPE is unresponsive.

ISABELLA: Perhaps Maestro, we should let you rest; all the travelling – you must be tired….

FARINELLI: I am not fond of sleep. *(He picks up the music that PHILIPPE dropped.)*

(To PHILIPPE.) Your Majesty, I have a gift for you… I was given it in London… I think you might like it.

The intro to the aria begins: 'Fra Tempeste Funeste' from 'Rodelinda' by Handel (A section only).

The SINGER appears in the doorway; he is bearing a telescope – it is clearly a very expensive gift. He brings the telescope to FARINELLI… FARINELLI gives it to PHILIPPE who stares at it lifelessly… The SINGER causes the stars to descend… FARINELLI puts the telescope to PHILIPPE's eye… PHILIPPE is amazed at what he sees… CERVI and LA CUADRA enter, anxious, ready for violence, but find PHILIPPE looking through a telescope… PHILIPPE gives the telescope to ISABELLA like a gesture of thank you for what she's done, kisses her, leaves her and gestures to CERVI and LA CUADRA (amazed) to leave the chamber. The three of them exit. FARINELLI and ISABELLA look through the telescope together. She leaves, with a smile at FARINELLI; the SINGER asks for the telescope back… FARINELLI obeys, and the SINGER places the telescope carefully on a table... The SINGER commands the stars to rise... Both SINGER and FARINELLI exit – but for a brief moment, face each other before we see them disappear.

SCENE 6. THE PALACE, MADRID.

Late morning. Three weeks later. An antechamber

PHILIPPE and LA CUADRA enter with MIGUEL, who bears a flask of wine and fills a glass for PHILIPPE.

PHILIPPE: So you think I should go to France – to beg!

LA CUADRA: Dr Cervi tells me you are much restored.

PHILIPPE: Are you mad?

LA CUADRA: The last few weeks have confirmed his opinion.

PHILIPPE: So now you think I'm well enough, you want me to pop off to Paris.

LA CUADRA: We feel, it is a question of...visibility. You are family.

PHILIPPE: You want me to be visibly supporting my nephew's marriage to his Polish Queen. God. If I had to tackle up for that every night –

LA CUADRA: This morning I received this – *(Puts a letter down in front of PHILIPPE.)* – our Ambassador in London says the English ships have sailed; We are on the brink of war.

PHILIPPE: Dear God. I mean, Poland! Where is it?

LA CUADRA: We need to get France back on side before England can attack: it's a question of...visibility: the King of Spain needs to be seen.

PHILIPPE: Oh does he. By whom?

LA CUADRA: The people of France. And Spain.

PHILIPPE: Why? Have you asked them?

LA CUADRA: Well no, not exactly, but –

PHILIPPE: Then how the fuck do you know what they need?

LA CUADRA: It's my job, sir.

PHILIPPE: – do they need me to parade out on the balcony in my birthday suit? Showing off my bollocks? Will that help France or Spain?

LA CUADRA: Your Majesty, we cannot afford another war; France can protect us – she is your home –

PHILIPPE: – War is war. It will happen despite alliances.

LA CUADRA: Dr Cervi would agree that a journey to the French court –

PHILIPPE: Oh you'd like that, wouldn't you, La Cuadra! I see it now, jollying along in the Royal coach, picking up the odd prostitute on the way to keep you happy and arriving in Paris with the clap – well I don't know about you, but I can't see the Queen warming to that idea.

LA CUADRA: The Queen will not accompany us.

PHILIPPE: I suspect she wouldn't. She'd rather boil her head in oil. No, we're all staying here with Farinelli.

LA CUADRA: Signor Farinelli could accompany you.

PHILIPPE: Approve of him now, do you?

LA CUADRA: His…effect…has been beneficial –

PHILIPPE: Beneficial? Not for your priests and exorcists!

LA CUADRA: Sire – we need to get your family back on side before England can attack: time's run out!

PHILIPPE: Get Farinelli for me.

LA CUADRA: He has been singing late into the night.

PHILIPPE: Well I've been kinging late into the night. Get him. *(LA CUADRA exits. Under his breath:)* Dear God.

ISABELLA enters. She is carrying some large plans, rolled up.

ISABELLA: What are these?

PHILIPPE: Oh – I have been thinking about the stars.

ISABELLA: What?

PHILIPPE: I want to hear them.

ISABELLA: You want to hear the stars.

PHILIPPE: Yes.

ISABELLA: You can't hear stars.

PHILIPPE: You can in a forest.

ISABELLA: How do you know?

He looks at her but says nothing.

PHILIPPE: We're going to live in a forest.

ISABELLA: What?

PHILIPPE: I'm going to build a house in a forest.

ISABELLA: You've already built a house in a forest.

PHILIPPE: That's *next* to a forest. Not *in*. That one's too big.

ISABELLA: But –

PHILIPPE: And there are too many servants.

ISABELLA: That's ridiculous. There's half the number of –

PHILIPPE: – We don't need them.

ISABELLA: I'm just trying to understand why –

PHILIPPE: I want to live in a forest. That's all. I want to cut a hole in the forest –

ISABELLA: You want to *what*?

PHILIPPE: – so I can look up and hear the stars. I want to hear the hidden notes.

ISABELLA: Hidden notes?

PHILIPPE: The music of the spheres, he says. I have been trying, but I can't.

ISABELLA: Spheres?

PHILIPPE: It's up there. *(Points to the sky outside.)* The sound of a relationship.

ISABELLA: Oh.

PHILIPPE: Two notes, an interval. Music between one planet and another, Farinelli told me.

ISABELLA: He did, did he…

PHILIPPE: – It's there. Animals can hear it; their ears are attuned so sensitively.

ISABELLA: Well they may, but –

PHILIPPE: Am I animal enough, do you think, Isabella?

ISABELLA: But this is ridiculous. We have a retreat.

PHILIPPE: – it's about the numbers.

ISABELLA: Numbers?

PHILIPPE: Yes.

ISABELLA: What is?

PHILIPPE: *(Tries to make it clear, as if to a child of three.)* Planets. Vibrating. Each one spins out a series of numbers, you see.

ISABELLA: I don't quite.

PHILIPPE: Notes are vibrations at several hundred times a second. Numbers. The music of the spheres. All vibrating at different rates – A, B, Gb – When he sings a note, he says, it includes the sound of other notes, notes which we individually cannot hear but are offshoots – like children – isn't that extraordinary? Think of it, Isabella.

ISABELLA: I am thinking. Definitely thinking that I am not going to live in a forest with a hole cut in it.

PHILIPPE: He calls them harmonics. *(Under his breath.)* Cervi knows about them.

ISABELLA: Harmonics? What are –

PHILIPPE: – They're up there. Here. Everywhere. It's become so clear. To listen for the music of the spheres. I get a glimpse of it when he sings to me. I think this might be why I am feeling better.

ISABELLA: Well why can't we just open the windows –

PHILIPPE: – This is an experiment. Science.

ISABELLA: But in the gardens –

PHILIPPE: – He needs to sing where it is natural where it is quiet enough.

ISABELLA: But –why not just make it very very quiet here? You only have to say, and they –

PHILIPPE: – Aren't you funny! *(He is affectionate with her.)*

We will live there together, You, me, and Farinelli.

The children can visit. But as they are noisy, I will choose visiting times.

ISABELLA: But what about our duty here?

PHILIPPE: La Cuadra.

ISABELLA: Oh God, You can't.

PHILIPPE: Think of it; at night, we will work hard to hear the music of the heavens. We will be rewarded, I have no doubt.

ISABELLA: But you are the King! You can't just leave Madrid at this time!

PHILIPPE: If you love me, and because it is your duty, you will live with me there too. And you will take part in the experiment. Because you are animal enough. *(He suddenly finds her very very sexy.)*

ISABELLA: *(She is floored.)* But… Who will dress us? Cook –

PHILIPPE: I'll undress you. *(He suddenly finds her very very sexy.)*

(Starts to undress her. She tries to dress herself as he undresses her but finds it difficult without help.) Can you not dress yourself? It's time you learned. And there are books to teach you cookery. We will all try. Very hard. *(He's all over her.)*

ISABELLA: But – Farinelli… He won't want to live in a wood! – It'll all go wrong… Just when – *(She bursts into tears.)*

PHILIPPE: Oh no, no no little Mouse! – You see…you are a very lovely and desirable woman, but you must have air and flowers and beauty around you. You see – *(he grabs the ground plan)* on this ground plan – …this is what I am imagining for us – see how I've drawn it? Here is your parlour, where I will cover the ceiling with stars so that we shall never be without them… Yes…and here – look – we will make a natural garden full of wildflowers. We will hear our music outside – and we will be in conversation with the heavens… – and you can make onion soup like my dear wife Marie Louise used to make for me –

ISABELLA: I don't like onion soup.

PHILIPPE: I am happy, for the first time in my life. Would you deny me that?

ISABELLA: No. No.

PHILIPPE: You would. You wish me to stay here, in this chamber of horrors, caged up like an animal.

ISABELLA: No, no of course I don't.

PHILIPPE: *(Dangerously.)* – You want to keep me here so you can run my country.

ISABELLA: No, that's not right. Or at least –

PHILIPPE tears up all the charts.

ISABELLA: Oh. Please don't.

PHILIPPE: So cruel. All of you. It'll come back.

Pause.

ISABELLA: I'm sorry. So sorry. Please. *(She kneels down and tries to put the charts back together again.)*

PHILIPPE: I love you and yet you torture me.

ISABELLA: I didn't think.

PHILIPPE: It doesn't matter now.

ISABELLA: It *does* matter. Very much. What you need.

PHILIPPE: You need me to stay here. I can't.

ISABELLA: I'm here with you. *(She kisses him tenderly.)* And I'll be part of it…your…experiment.

PHILIPPE: There is no experiment. It's gone. You killed it.

FARINELLI enters. Unseen by them.

ISABELLA: of course there will be an experiment. I promise. I will make onion soup for you. I will make it better than she did. *(Sees FARINELLI.)* – Oh Carlo! Come and look at this. *(Indicates the pieces of drawing.)* We're leaving Madrid. We're going to live in a forest.

FARINELLI: Oh. *(Beat.)* It seems then, it is my time to leave you.

PHILIPPE: You can't. I'm still not well.

ISABELLA: You are to be an experiment.

PHILIPPE: It's more than that.

ISABELLA: He will tell you.

PHILIPPE: Do you like trees?

FARINELLI: What?

PHILIPPE: Do you like living in forests?

FARINELLI: I don't know.

PHILIPPE: You're going to.

FARINELLI: And the experiment?

ISABELLA: You are to sing.

FARINELLI: To whom?

PHILIPPE: To the stars of course. We're going to have a conversation with them. Just us; you and me. And Isabella will cook... *(He sees her face and moves on.)* Miguel! We are going to learn to hear, and hunt for answers. *(He throws off his sash and coat and dumps them on a chair, puts wig on MIGUEL's head.)* We'll leave these selves behind; where we're going has no time for Kings, or angels with knives. So, Farinelli, sing us a farewell to Madrid – and for God's sake make it a happy one!

The 'spirit of the forest' (the SINGER) flies in singing 'Sento la Gioia' from 'Amadigi di Gaula' by Handel (A section only): the SINGER, dressed in the true operatic style FARINELLI may have once worn, is throwing glitter as he descends...

PHILIPPE gleefully exits with ISABELLA. FARINELLI stares upwards at the 'spirit of the forest' before following after them; the stage is left to the SINGER alone as the transformation is effected in an entirely theatrical way: we are now in the Forest with a hole cut in it.

End of ACT ONE.

INTERVAL

ACT TWO

SCENE 1.
THE FOREST OUTSIDE SAN IDLEFONSO, AUGUST 26TH 1737.

Music (Aria: 'Se in Fiorito' from 'Giulio Cesare' by Handel. A section only), during which:

A clearing in the forest. FARINELLI is trying to garden, without success; the SINGER enters – the aria begins. The SINGER is encouraging FARINELLI. ISABELLA enters carrying a basket – she is on her way to collect vegetables. She pauses to pluck an apple from a tree hung with golden apples: she takes a bite: they are both arrested by the sound of a beautiful bird (echoing the SINGER's call with an identical one of its own)… ISABELLA looks over FARINELLI's shoulder at his efforts to garden – nothing is registering in the earth. She sighs in sympathy and moves away. FARINELLI loses all patience and throws all the seeds in to the hole he has dug, and walks away, frustrated. The aria pauses, the music stops. Something strange and wonderful is in the air: FARINELLI turns and sees – a garden of flowers has sprung up exactly where he has been gardening (through the trap in the stage floor)! He is overjoyed and thrilled! The SINGER leaves triumphantly, taking the tree with him. The aria ends.

RICH: Why?

When the world is at your feet, why would you run for the back door, and disappear?

This isn't what I planned. We're pissing off a lot of people. He's on contract. He's supposed to be back within the month. I've even had his house painted. That's set me back a bit. Now I get this: *(Indicates in the letter he is holding.)*

FARINELLI: 'What peace in my heart I have found amongst these people. This new life has helped me bid a fond Farewell to Farinelli; he is gone the way of old productions. Here the music springs from a different well; it quenches not the thirst for entertainment but the melancholy of my friend the King.'

RICH: 'My friend the King!'

FARINELLI: 'He is decidedly better because of me, and in his lonely life I have become a song he now depends on.'

RICH: Well that's great. Because he's a song that *I* depend on, and he's hiding out in some wood in Spain when he should be here. In London. Where he belongs! Our audiences are dwindling to nothing. The Beggar's Opera is on its last legs. Jokes and anecdotes, that's all I've got for them now. And I've always been shite at those.

FARINELLI: 'We are taking part in an extraordinary experiment exploring the communion between the soul and the body and the influence of the planets of Jupiter, with Mercury and Venus. Tonight, we ran outside to see if all three planets were visible in the night sky; and to the King's delight, they were! And now we are getting ready for a very rare.'

RICH: 'Eclipse of the sun!'

FARINELLI: 'PS: I am sending you a packet of vanilla, chocolate and extract of amaranth, which I know you will relish; the King's succeeded in making me give up the sweet stuff.' *(Exits.)*

RICH: So there we are. The world's greatest opera singer now performing to an audience of one. He tells me it's been a hot summer but the garden's doing fine apart from the slugs.

He exits, closing the trap on the garden of flowers as he does so.

LA CUADRA and DR CERVI arrive from the forest with MIGUEL.

LA CUADRA: We're going around in circles. It's ridiculous; indefensible: the King of Spain living in the middle of a forest! No bloody roads. Just mud. Where are we?

CERVI: But the air's good here. This is the perfect place.

LA CUADRA: Hmph. Miguel. Find out where the hell we are. *(MIGUEL goes off.)* I can't have this country made a laughing stock. It's time the King was back. I need him in Madrid.

CERVI: The King may not be ready.

LA CUADRA: It is my hope, Doctor Cervi, that he will be. If you say he is.

CERVI: Even if I think him fit, he may not want to return –

LA CUADRA: It's not a question of what he wants but what Spain needs!

CERVI: Spain needs the King to be well.

LA CUADRA: He *must* return.

CERVI: To pack him off to war? I don't advise it.

LA CUADRA: There'll be a revolution.

CERVI: Against the King?

LA CUADRA: The harvest has failed again.

CERVI: The King is not to blame for that!

LA CUADRA: People are fickle. They turn on an instant. Their King is absent, chasing fireflies in a forest, when he should be doing the job God gave him.

CERVI: Are you suggesting –

LA CUADRA: A republic? It's happened before. And it will happen again. Europe is changing.

CERVI: He may collapse if we take him back with us.

LA CUADRA: Test him.

CERVI: What?

LA CUADRA: Test him. Put him under pressure. You'll find a way.

ISABELLA enters with a huge basket filled with vegetables. Her hair is undone and her face smudged with earth.

Ah. Ma'am.

ISABELLA: Senor La Cuadra. Dr Cervi!

LA CUADRA: Word has it his that the King is restored to – a happier state of mind. Would you agree? *(He takes the heavy basket from her.)*

ISABELLA: His humour seems stable. Have you come to see for yourself?

LA CUADRA: I have brought Dr Cervi with me.

ISABELLA: I see. Yes. What an unexpected pleasure. *(CERVI kisses her hand.)*

CERVI: The pleasure is mine.

LA CUADRA: I have come to collect his Majesty. He must return with me.

ISABELLA: Why?

LA CUADRA: You came for a month. It's been three.

ISABELLA: Not quite.

LA CUADRA: He's missed the Festival of the Assumption.

ISABELLA: How dull.

LA CUADRA: And an emergency convening of the Council.

ISABELLA: Are we now at war, La Cuadra? Is that what you're really saying?

LA CUADRA: That is no concern of yours Ma'am.

ISABELLA: Don Sebastian, I am not a child you can frighten; I was born to smell a war from my cradle.

Pause.

LA CUADRA: Well then, you won't like the smell of the English ships – they're formidable.

ISABELLA: But talks with Britain?

LA CUADRA: Broken down. Irrevocably.

ISABELLA: Well then, it's clear. You need us back.

LA CUADRA: I need the *King* back. But you must remain here.

There is plague in the city. The Summer –

ISABELLA: I have an iron constitution. The King does not.

LA CUADRA: The King has an heir, should the worst happen.

ISABELLA: *(Laughs.)* Don Sebastian! But the real reason, is, as you and I both know, that as the King's second wife I am unpopular. That won't help your cause.

LA CUADRA: Well I –

ISABELLA: *This* Queen will not help you rally the people. To persuade them to sign up for another bout of bloodshed. Isn't that it?

PHILIPPE enters. He looks well and has been gardening.

PHILIPPE: La Cuadra! Dr Cervi! Visitors, Isabella! You must stay for supper. It's casserole. *(To LA CUADRA.)* That's French, for – paella.

Oh – *(Seeing the vegetables which LA CUADRA is still holding.)* You've picked them!

ISABELLA: They were perfectly ready.

PHILIPPE: You shouldn't have. It's not right.

ISABELLA: To pick them?

PHILIPPE: *(To LA CUADRA.)* Did you ask them? *(To ISABELLA.)* Did he ask them?

ISABELLA: No of course not!

PHILIPPE: Vegetables have rights, dear. Look at them. Now I'll have to plant some more in the gap, so the asparagus doesn't feel outflanked. Those blackberries are fully armed and getting very aggressive. *(Exits.)*

ISABELLA: You see how it is. Now… I must invite you to our amusements before supper. The King wants Farinelli to sing outside. You will be our guest of honour. He's going to sing a Handel aria just for you. I hope you will enjoy it. Did you know that London has built a new Opera House? *(She takes the trug from LA CUADRA.)*

CERVI: Oh!

LA CUADRA: *(Sotto voce.)* Hrmph.

ISABELLA: Yes; opera's so popular, everywhere now. Perhaps *our people* will turn to it when this terrible love of war will tire. I must get on. Please excuse me Dr Cervi.

She exits.

LA CUADRA, determined, looks after her.

LA CUADRA: It's in her blood. She'll be pouring money into an opera house which the Spanish will hate. There'll be no Italians making opera in Spain. We are for bull fights and honest street theatre: good family entertainment that sees us getting to our beds at a decent time of the night.

CERVI: Well, sleep is –

LA CUADRA: Spain is a nation of farmers and soldiers, we will not piss away what little money we have on idle warblers!

CERVI: Oh but don't you think –

LA CUADRA: No, Dr Cervi, 'the opera' will never be 'popular' in Spain…I will wager everything I have on that!

Music. The sound of tuning up.

LA CUADRA: Bloody hell! What's that racket!

CERVI: They're tuning up. Rehearsing.

CERVI is thinking.

LA CUADRA: I can't hear myself think! *(Pulls out a shot flask.)*

CERVI: You go in; I need the air. I'll join you in a moment.

LA CUADRA: God knows what we'll get to eat here. *(Sotte voce.)* Nothing but turnips, I imagine.

They exit, LA CUADRA into the house, CERVI into the forest away from the house.

The tuning up gets more musical, more vigorous and then tails away.

SCENE 2. A LITTLE LATER.

PHILIPPE and FARINELLI enter from the gardens… They are carrying footlights, music stands and paraphernalia to arrange on the 'stage' for the concert…

PHILIPPE: Look Farinelli! Our clearing.

FARINELLI: It's as bright as day!

PHILIPPE: It's the moon. She shines so well.

FARINELLI: This clearing…it looks as if it's always been here.

PHILIPPE: It'll be perfect for your singing. Listen. The spiders are dismantling their webs. They sense it.

FARINELLI: The eclipse?

PHILIPPE: No! Your singing.

FARINELLI: Will it change us, this eclipse?

PHILIPPE: Why? Would you like to have red hair?

FARINELLI: NO!

PHILIPPE: Would you like to go home?

FARINELLI: No.

PHILIPPE: Do you understand Italian?

FARINELLI: Of course I do!

PHILIPPE: I don't. Not a word.

FARINELLI: So you don't understand me when I sing! –

PHILIPPE: It's better that way. Do you understand birdsong?

FARINELLI: I don't speak bird. But I get the gist. 'This tree's mine.'

PHILIPPE: Exactly. Have you ever been in love?

FARINELLI: Almost.

PHILIPPE: I have loved two women. One was as delicate as a sapling; the other –

Do you think my wife is wild or cultivated?

FARINELLI: I've not thought –

PHILIPPE: She's as cultivated as a box hedge and as wild as a bear! When the moon is full she is marvelous.

FARINELLI looks round and sees a lot of people seemingly spilling out from the trees…

FARINELLI: Who are all these people?

PHILIPPE: Farinelli! Have you gone mad? It's just trees! *(He gets a small pair of glasses from his pocket and puts them on.)* Oh my God!

FARINELLI: Look, they're all sitting down, now!

PHILIPPE: There she is! Over here, Isabella!

SCENE 3. CONTINUOUS.

ISABELLA arrives, with LA CUADRA and DR CERVI in tow.

PHILIPPE: Who are they, Isabella?

ISABELLA: I don't know.

PHILIPPE: We didn't expect others here.

ISABELLA: They seem to be the local townspeople –

PHILIPPE: – then it's a bloody big town.

LA CUADRA: This is turning public. Call it off.

ISABELLA: The ground is rather hard, but they seem not to mind it.

FARINELLI: And still more arrive… I –

PHILIPPE: – They are not afraid of the earth, nor of their bodies; they don't hide from nature as we do. There is no shame of their desires amongst them.

Look Isabella, our gardener and his family! What sweet little children!

ISABELLA: If rather grubby.

FARINELLI: – I think, if you don't mind, I –

ISABELLA: – Do you mind singing for them, just once? They have so little –

PHILIPPE: – Don't let her push you, Farinelli, I don't mind either way. It's awkward though. Here they are. All looking expectant and we've got fuck all for them.

ISABELLA: We'll have to do something.

CERVI: *(To PHILIPPE.)* Why don't you speak to them?

LA CUADRA: I don't think that's a good idea.

PHILIPPE: Well then. *(He puts his glasses back in his pocket.)* Good evening everyone. *(To the audience, and off the cuff.)* This morning, I was given back a memory which had been stolen from me; I was a small boy once again with my grandfather, walking in the gardens of Versailles. How I hated those formal gardens of his! Small boys want to climb trees steal apples from their boughs, and think bad thoughts about the chamber maids! No place for any of that in the gardens of Louis XIV. I longed for freedom, to tear my clothes off and jump into one of those ornamental ponds…one day I did it! My father the Dauphin was apoplectic! So why this memory? A young boy jumping naked into the fountain, the cold water splashing over my genitals…it made me ecstatic with joy, desire, longing all at once for the things I did not have…and then the beating… in another country, another ten year old would have his balls cut off in order to acquire the very thing that now gives me all my joy…and so around we go; pain, joy, ecstasy, despair. Now I feel, I hear, I see. And do you know, how this elusive memory of mine came back to me? Sleeping in this garden I dreamed an angel was singing to me, – and this was you, Farinelli – and when I woke up, there I knew myself again in that fountain in Versailles – the place where I was born, – and now – *(To a man in the audience.)* Aren't you the poacher? I admire the way you steal my pheasants. I've seen you. Under the dark moon. Don't think I don't know you do…you're lucky not to be hanged! Any other King would have hung you…but as you amuse me…would you like to come to supper? We…

ISABELLA: – Your musicians are assembling.

PHILIPPE: – An assembly of musicians! Ha! A shoal of sheep, a herd of maggots, *(Looks at the cellist's beard.)* A congress of fleas, a pride of dodos… Farinelli, tell the people about opera.

FARINELLI: People coming to see me fail the top notes. It's a freak show.

PHILIPPE: Now I am interested. I myself am that. I find myself curious about the Opera. What is it?

LA CUADRA: It belongs to another world.

PHILIPPE: So do I. Tell us about it.

LA CUADRA: Stories. Sung. That's all.

ISABELLA: No, no far more than that!

PHILIPPE: Farinelli, I hear even in London they have built another opera house in a garden of some convent.

ISABELLA: Well, the opera house in The Haymarket is magical; but no more harmful than a child's toy; In front of the stage, people are standing, packed together like smoked herrings in a box; ladies in fine clothes leaning forward from their seats or standing, craning to get a better look at you. *(FARINELLI half goes to sit…)*

PHILIPPE: No, no… *(FARINELLI gets up.)* Tell us: what does it smell like?

FARINELLI: Hundreds of candles mixed with human sweat… the catgut and horsehair of the violins…breath of the wind players. And boys spreading pomanders about the place to try and make it smell better.

LA CUADRA: Horrible.

PHILIPPE: *(Enjoying it.)* So they smell terrible but what are they doing, packed together like that? What do they expect?

ISABELLA: A Story. They've come for the story.

PHILIPPE: Well haven't we all! *(Indicating the audience.)*

LA CUADRA: Stories can be dangerous:

PHILIPPE: (*To FARINELLI.)* Tell us the story of the first time you ever sang in an opera house.

FARINELLI: Oh… I don't remember.

ISABELLA: Your London debut! Tell us about that!

FARINELLI: On my first London appearance, I sang an opera composed by my brother Riccardo –

PHILIPPE: – Ricc the knife –

FARINELLI: – yes, that one. The people had heard about me in advance, so when I came on to the stage I… *(He falters. Stops.)*

CERVI: Tell us what you were wearing. How were you dressed?

FARINELLI: Full armour. It was impossible for me to see because of this helmet I was wearing –

PHILIPPE: – you can never see properly out of those wretched things – go on –

FARINELLI: I felt something crunching under my feet and I managed to get a glimpse of what I was walking on…and it was a carpet of flowers; thousands of roses –

ISABELLA: – the audience had thrown!

FARINELLI: Yes. I worried for my throat in case it swelled, because the scent was so strong. *(He stops. Feels his throat.)*

PHILIPPE: *(Encouragingly.)* Throats can do that with some flowers. What happened then?

FARINELLI: They had to play the introduction twice, there was so much screaming. I couldn't hear the orchestra. *(He stops.)*

LA CUADRA: It sounds vicious. Animals feasting on meat.

FARINELLI: My brother was conducting. He was waiting for me to begin. I couldn't. I looked at all their expectant faces. I opened my mouth but no sound came out. I stood there like a fool, silent and terrified. They started to jeer. Throw fruit. Even old shoes. I looked at my brother. This meant everything to him. He was staring back at me, startled, angry. I felt blank. Out of nowhere I heard a high note in the air. I wondered where it was coming from. I realized it was me. I went on to sing the aria, but none of the notes belonged to me; they belonged only to him. At the end, the crowd erupted with cheers; called to my brother to come on stage. We bowed together, hand in hand. We were famous overnight. So he had what he wanted. Every night after that it was easy. I was being paid a fortune to perform on the high wire of the London opera stage. I dazzled them with ornaments and trills. But I felt nothing. Not even despair.

Pause.

PHILIPPE: My friend, if you sing for us we will listen. We will even shut our eyes if you like. We won't scream. And we won't pick the roses, will we.

FARINELLI: No. I – really don't – I can't –

Pause.

CERVI: There's a high note.

ISABELLA: Where?

CERVI: Up there. See it?

FARINELLI: What is that?

PHILIPPE: Venus. I think. Yes.

FARINELLI: Venus.

CERVI: You can see it through the hole in the forest.

ISABELLA: We're not in an opera house, we're in a forest!

FARINELLI: We're in a forest!

PHILIPPE: Sing. It will be different now.

Beat.

ISABELLA: Sing, Carlo. *(She holds out her hand to him.)*

He starts to sing: 'Venti Turbini' from 'Rinaldo' by Handel.

At the end of the aria there is enormous applause from the audience. PHILIPPE is applauding. The impromptu public opera has been a great triumph.

ISABELLA: So. You see, Don Sebastian, how much the people of Spain like to hear an opera.

LA CUADRA: It would seem so, Ma'am.

PHILIPPE: How did all these people hear about this? Was it you Isabella?

ISABELLA: No. It's a mystery to me.

PHILIPPE: La Cuadra?

LA CUADRA: No Sir.

PHILIPPE: What a pity. It might have been one of your better ideas. *(He exits, followed by LA CUADRA and FARINELLI, who hangs back. DR CERVI has been looking at where the audience was…and then goes to join the others…ISABELLA detains him.)*

ISABELLA: It was you, wasn't it. Who told the people. About tonight.

CERVI: And word spread.

CERVI bows and exits. ISABELLA looks after him, thinking hard.

FARINELLI appears next to ISABELLA.

SCENE 4. CONTINUOUS.

ISABELLA: So, Signor. Tonight has given me hope.

FARINELLI: It's beautiful out here. So still.

ISABELLA: You could see how happy the people were. When you sang –

FARINELLI: –you can see so many stars…

ISABELLA: So I thought –

FARINELLI: – The Milky Way is so clear. Who lives there I wonder.

ISABELLA: – They loved it so much, I thought we should build an opera house for them – what do you think?

FARINELLI: – Each planet talking to another; a sky full of music – Look. *(He points upward at the sky.)*

ISABELLA: What am I looking at?

FARINELLI: Ursa Minor. Just a bit more to your right. *(Guides her.)* Yes, like that.

ISABELLA: Ursa Minor. The Little Bear.

FARINELLI: See it?

ISABELLA: Yes I think so. Yes.

FARINELLI: And round it, the coils of Draco.

ISABELLA: Draco. The Dragon.

FARINELLI: Yes, see that?

ISABELLA: I'd be lying if I said I could. *(Trying.)* Why is it called that?

FARINELLI: The story goes that this Draco was thrown at the Goddess Minerva by the Giants, when she fought them. But she gathered up its twisted form and threw it to the stars.

ISABELLA: Oh!

FARINELLI: And there it is. *(He looks at her.)*

ISABELLA: There it is. *(She looks at him. She kisses him. He kisses her back. They pull apart.)*

ISABELLA: I love the King; do you know that? I thought that when he would be well again…then so should I…feel loved. But I do not. Feel loved.

FARINELLI: I know.

ISABELLA: When he was ill, I knew who he was. Now he is recovered – I don't know myself anymore. But should we not become well? But we must, and then what?

FARINELLI: There is no plan. No guide.

ISABELLA: *(She takes his hand.)* These past months here… We have become very close, the three of us.

FARINELLI: Yes.

ISABELLA: Does this feel untrue? Do you deny that you desire me?

FARINELLI is very still.

ISABELLA: What do you think of me?

FARINELLI: I think you are the most beautiful woman I have ever met or seen.

ISABELLA: That is absurdly untrue.

FARINELLI: I do desire you. I do want you, to have you, now. But I cannot betray the King. You know that.

ISABELLA: 'That love allows nothing beloved to love another'.

FARINELLI: '*Che amore a nullo amar perdona.*' It is a beautiful phrase.

ISABELLA: It is deadly. *(Pause. They look at each other. They daren't touch.)* The King is going back to Madrid – do you know that?

FARINELLI: What do you mean?

ISABELLA: That's why La Cuadra's here. To take him back.

FARINELLI: But the King is not recovered.

ISABELLA: Tonight, in the garden…he didn't panic; La Cuadra saw. Cervi. Philippe is ready to go back.

FARINELLI: No. His mind is still healing.

ISABELLA: He must return to Madrid. It is his duty.

FARINELLI: And you?

ISABELLA: I will go too. They don't want me to, but I will. *(Beat.)* Carlo, we will need you in Madrid. We will need you more than ever.

Pause.

FARINELLI: It is late. We are tired –

ISABELLA: You gave us hope. Remember?

FARINELLI: – I must leave you before we say things to each other we will regret.

ISABELLA: Carlo –

FARINELLI: We will talk in the morning.

(He takes her hand and looks at it.) What have you done to your hand?

ISABELLA: I burnt it. Cooking.

FARINELLI holds her hand close to his heart.

You love me, don't you. Say it.

FARINELLI is silent, still holding her hand.

Say it.

FARINELLI: Tonight. Singing for the people. For you. Thank you.

Drops her hand, leaves.

ISABELLA: Carlo –

'Cara Sposa' from 'Rinaldo' by Handel (B section only). An aria of love, longing and loneliness.

He walks away…walking slowly though trying to leave fast; wanting to stay; looking back at her all the while…until he is out of sight… she looks after him well after he disappears from sight…

SCENE 5

Later. PHILIPPE and ISABELLA.

PHILIPPE: He is leaving us.

ISABELLA: Yes.

PHILIPPE: You knew?

ISABELLA: No. Yes. At least –

PHILIPPE: At least?

ISABELLA: I thought he would.

PHILIPPE: Why did you not tell me?

ISABELLA: We thought it would upset you.

PHILIPPE: *We?!*

ISABELLA: And I thought –

PHILIPPE: You thought?! What did you think? That I am a child?

ISABELLA: No of course not.

Pause.

ISABELLA: Well… it's time to –

PHILIPPE: *Time*? Who are you to tell me about *time!* Do you think I am a child?

ISABELLA: No of course not –

PHILIPPE: I see you, see what you have done…been doing… playing me, all of you, playing me, like I am a game… I hate you for this…you have made him go, haven't you, to make me as I was…when you could…when I didn't know…and now…

ISABELLA: Shush shush, please. No one has been –

PHILIPPE: Plotting! All of you! Against me!

ISABELLA: No! Why would we?

PHILIPPE: Think I can't see it.

ISABELLA: See what?

PHILIPPE: Your heart – How it shines! Ah. Ah. Come here.

ISABELLA: I, I –

PHILIPPE kisses her violently on the mouth and bites her mouth through the kiss.

PHILIPPE: This is what you like, isn't it, this is what you understand!

She runs from him, her mouth streaming with blood.

DR CERVI enters

Animals. It's in her blood. We are all animals. Here is her blood. *(Tastes it.)* We can't help ourselves.

ISABELLA: *(From the forest.)* Cervi!

PHILIPPE: Cervi – You have to help me. You have to give me – something. To take away this… Before I… My mind is slipping into darkness; I feel it being pulled from me Slipping though I try to hold on… It is as thin as an eggshell –

CERVI: – It will not break.

PHILIPPE: It is the fear of breaking. I am frightened, Cervi. I beg you; give me something to take away the fear.

CERVI: There is no drug that will take away your fear. Only hold it at arms length.

PHILIPPE: I command you. *(He holds out his hand.)*

CERVI: I can't. *(Beat.)* I'm sorry.

CERVI exits

FARINELLI enters.

PHILIPPE: So! You are breaking your promise to me.

You promised never to leave me.

FARINELLI: Then I am sorry.

PHILIPPE: You are sorry. I am sorry. Cervi's sorry. The world is sorry.

FARINELLI: I will return. My heart is here.

PHILIPPE: Is it? What can I believe? Who can I trust?

FARINELLI: No one except yourself. And what you think and truly feel.

PHILIPPE: I am a King. We are not allowed to think or truly feel. We are grown that way from our beginnings.

FARINELLI: Even so. I believe you know in your own heart that you can trust me.

Beat.

PHILIPPE: Why are you going? You are needed here.

FARINELLI: And I shall return, I promise.

PHILIPPE: As soon as you are away you will forget about us here.

FARINELLI: No, I assure you I will not.

PHILIPPE: You will return to your old life, the opera.

FARINELLI: I have no intention of ever doing that.

PHILIPPE: They will make you offers you can't refuse.

FARINELLI: I am not open to offers.

PHILIPPE: I am lost without you. With her.

ISABELLA enters.

PHILIPPE: Isabella! Tell him he can't go! He must not leave us!

ISABELLA: *(To FARINELLI.)* Don't leave us.

FARINELLI: His Majesty's health is so much improved, that I feel I –

PHILIPPE: Improved! I shall never be that!

ISABELLA: You can't leave. You can see how it is.

PHILIPPE: I can command you to stay.

FARINELLI: If you love me, you will not.

PHILIPPE: I do not love you. I just desire you to sing. You must sing to me; in the long hours of dark, when my mind is screaming in the silence, then that is when I need you to sing to me. You know this and yet you abandon me!

FARINELLI is silent.

ISABELLA: Dawn flowers are so very pretty after the rain... but they rarely live past sunset. *(She realizes her lip is still bleeding. She wipes it away.)*

FARINELLI: Would you both excuse me? I must review the arrangements they are making for my travel... *(He exits.)*

ISABELLA: I had thought...that tonight, after supper –

PHILIPPE: – Tonight? I may not live that long!

ISABELLA: – you could tell us the history of your family's rule in Spain.

PHILIPPE: I do not like to be reminded of history.

ISABELLA: I –

PHILIPPE: Which is why I need him to sing to me.

ISABELLA: But I –

PHILIPPE: His voice reminds me that it is possible to live in this world; a miracle indeed when there are people such as you in it who would wish me out of it.

ISABELLA: Why would you think that I would wish you out of it?

PHILIPPE: Because you do not love me. I don't blame you.

ISABELLA: But I do love you.

PHILIPPE: This *(pointing to his head)* is dying. Get out while you can.

Pause.

ISABELLA: La Cuadra tells me everything is ready for tomorrow.

PHILIPPE: Yes. *(Realizes she is talking about something.)* What?

ISABELLA: For Madrid.

PHILIPPE: It will kill me to go back to Madrid now. You know that.

ISABELLA: But I will be with you.

PHILIPPE: You know I am not better. Without Farinelli, it will be as before. Worse. Because now I know he is in the world and yet not here.

ISABELLA: He will return to us, some day. And then our life can really begin.

PHILIPPE: But my life began here in the forest, watching the leaves turn and fall from the bough; I have started to hear the stars, just a glimmer in my ear, an echo from the night sky…oh… And *you* would send me back *there*, to the Councils of war; where there is nothing for me but killing. Why would you do that?

ISABELLA: You are the King; a great king; you shone in battle and you will do so again, for me and for your country. And for your Grandfather, to show –

PHILIPPE: – I do not wish to speak of him! You know I can't bear…!

ISABELLA: Shhh! We will return here… I promise. Often. And Farinelli will come back. He will.

PHILIPPE: He won't. Our bird has flown.

ISABELLA: You have not eaten. Let me –

PHILIPPE: – I want to eat nothing, see no one. I only want his singing.

ISABELLA: We will eat together. Sleep together. So you won't be afraid.

PHILIPPE: Isabella.

ISABELLA: Yes…

PHILIPPE: If I go back, without him, I won't escape it again.

ISABELLA: I see.

PHILIPPE: So you do. It is not safe to go back without Farinelli so I am staying where it is safe until he returns to me.

Beat.

I am staying in my house in the forest, where it's safe, until he returns to me. Do you understand?

ISABELLA: Yes. *(Pause.)* It feels cold out here. We'll need a fire indoors. I'll see to it –

PHILIPPE: For God's sake! No fire!

PHILIPPE exits. FARINELLI enters.

FARINELLI: You have cut your lip.

ISABELLA: I will miss the music so much – did I say that before? My mother loved music –

FARINELLI: Did he hit you?

ISABELLA: – and we all learned to sing…except I never could. I –

FARINELLI: Leave him. Leave this place –

ISABELLA: – I have something for you.

FARINELLI: You are not safe here.

ISABELLA: *(It is a small bird in a tiny cage, all made from jewels. It is exquisite.)* Do you like it?… It sings. You just have to wind it up… *(They both look at it.)*

I hope it will remind you of your time here.

FARINELLI: I will not need reminding.

ISABELLA: And they say it was Farinelli that helped to restore the health of the King of Spain – just by hearing this wonderful singing voice the King rose out of his depression and wanted to live again!

FARINELLI: Come with me. Leave this.

ISABELLA: It was the only thing the King could bear in the end. The sound of Farinelli's voice.

FARINELLI: I say again. Come with me.

ISABELLA: Why? Where could I go?

FARINELLI: To a better place.

ISABELLA: My life is not a fable, Signor. I am the Queen. I must stay with my husband the King. You understand that. It is my duty. So farewell.

FARINELLI: I can't leave you here.

ISABELLA: I thank you. I have everything in order. I wish you well on your way.

FARINELLI: Isabella!

ISABELLA: I can have no need of you, Signor. But I thank you all the same.

PHILIPPE enters. He looks distracted. He is shading his eyes as if the light is too intense.

PHILIPPE: I can't sleep.

FARINELLI: My ship sails tomorrow morning early.

PHILIPPE: Well go if you're going. Don't make a meal of it.

FARINELLI: I won't. I have made my decision.

PHILIPPE: Decision. Incision.

Pause.

FARINELLI: I have decided to stay. If you will have me.

PHILIPPE: Oh. *(Beat.)* Now he wants to stay.

FARINELLI: Until the Spring.

PHILIPPE: Spring.

FARINELLI: And then in the Spring I must leave.

ISABELLA: Yes of course. *(Beat.)* In the Spring you must leave. And I'll talk with La Cuadra. He will give you everything you need.

PHILIPPE: You'll sing for me through the winter.

ISABELLA: Just until the Spring.

PHILIPPE: Good. Good. Now we can pretend you never wished to go away.

ISABELLA: *(To PHILIPPE.)* Your Farinelli will not leave you, he has promised... Oh it's cold; the weather has turned... *(She exits.)*

PHILIPPE: So. Farinelli. Tomorrow we shall be returning to Madrid. Our cottage here will soon be taken by voles and field mice for their home. These trees will grow a canopy to hide the hole we cut, and fold their sealing branches to exclude the moon. We are to war; there's no escaping that. So... Sing us from this starry wood – anything; the same piece if you like. Over and over. I need you to sing to me forever or until there is no life left in me...

He closes his eyes. Music starts. SINGER starts to sing 'Bel Contento' contento' from 'Flavio re de' Lombardi' by Handel. During the aria (which is interrupted), LA CUADRA, with DR CERVI enters with PHILIPPE's clothes, wig, sword and armour to prepare him for war; PHILIPPE – as if asleep – is dressed (by servants, supervised by LA CUADRA and DR CERVI) as he appears in the portrait of himself on a horse in Act One; the actor FARINELLI is detached, watching – then takes the Royal Sash from LA CUADRA and places it gently over PHILIPPE's shoulders. Towards the end of the aria, a lifesize wooden horse – as exactly in the painting – is pushed on to the stage. PHILIPPE is helped up on to the horse and LA CUADRA and

DR CERVI exit. PHILIPPE on the horse exits backwards… As the SINGER and FARINELLI also seem to 'melt' away (as he exits, his voice fades)…

JOHN RICH – twenty-two years older – enters the stage from the auditorium. Time jump…

SCENE 6. 1759. (TIME JUMP)

London. Covent Garden Theatre.

…we are onstage. A dress rehearsal of an opera. JOHN RICH claps his hands.

RICH: And… Exit the King… Good…and…we'll do Tenducci's aria now, boys, so brace yourselves. *(Band catcalls – they can't stand him.)*

(Calls.) Maestro Tenducci!

Beat.

Tenducci!

Stage manager (JETHRO who seems not to have aged much at all) appears.

JETHRO: He says he says he can't sing.

RICH: I know he can't sing but he's all we've got.

JETHRO: Sore throat.

RICH: What? Sore throat?

JETHRO: He says it's the weather. England. Too damp for him he says.

RICH: Opera singers! Bunch of tossers! What the hell are we going to do tonight?

JETHRO: I don't know guv'. Borrow someone. Guadagni?

RICH: Guadagni?! Guadagni's an animal. *(The band echoes that.)* He can't get anywhere near the top notes. Oh what difference will it make. Alright everyone, break for supper. *(Band cheer.)* Yes, yes, off you go, see you tonight, don't get drunk – oh, and speed up the tempo please otherwise we'll all be here past midnight. And I'm not paying overtime, so don't try it on. *(Aside.)* Dickheads! *(To JETHRO.)* – Oh Jethro, bring me my port would you. And some food, one of those – those new things – two pieces of bread with a bit of meat in the middle –

JETHRO: Sandwich.

RICH: Yeah… *(He sits down on a prop. He suddenly looks tired and old.)* Sore throat. Won't sing because it's damp. Bloody Italians. What's the point of them? Priscilla's said as much and she was right, bless her. 'We should pack the whole lot off to the continent, John. Get some of our money back, John.' She was right, they're not doing me any good here, and that's a fact.

ISABELLA enters, heavily veiled and dressed in black. She rolls back her veil and looks out at the auditorium.

RICH: *(In his peripheral vision, thinks it's the stagehand with the sandwich.)* Just put it down there, will you. *(Looks up.)* Oh! Dear Majesty! *(Bows.)* I had no idea you were coming! But – *(Looks at her black mourning clothing.)*

ISABELLA: *(Still looking out at the auditorium.)* – no, I'm not coming to the performance tonight. I wish I could.

RICH: – I heard of the King's… I am sorry for your loss. It must –

ISABELLA: Yes. Everything changes. So. Here you are… *(Still looking out.)*

RICH: The Covent Garden Theatre. The Square of Venus, they call it.

ISABELLA: *(Smiles, remembering.)* Venus. *(Beat.)* We built an opera house in Madrid. Farinelli and I…for the people…

He didn't sing in it, of course...How many does this hold? ...Five hundred?

RICH: Five hundred! No, Ma'am, it holds over a thousand. Princes and Duchesses under the same roof as road-menders and prostitutes; this is what I believe in; for the price of an orange –

ISABELLA: – anyone can hear the greatest music, the rarest voices.

Yes, that's wonderful.

RICH: And then the loveliest voice of all was taken away and put in a golden cage – *(ISABELLA continues to look into the auditorium as if she is imagining something and only half listening to him.)*

ISABELLA: Like a bird. Exactly like a bird.

RICH: Distracted by treats from a king's table, when he could have been singing here. For his people.

ISABELLA: He wanted to serve. But this is his natural kingdom.

RICH: Forgive my roughness, your Majesty. I – we have missed him; there is no one like him.

ISABELLA: Well that's good, for I want you to take him back.

Pause.

Spain is over for him. For us.

RICH: I don't understand. How –

ISABELLA: He must return here; he should never have come to Spain.

RICH: I still don't –

ISABELLA: Write to him. Win his heart. He cannot stay where I am. Without the King.

RICH: I see. *(Beat.)*

ISABELLA: Do you? *(Beat.)* Our new King doesn't like him. Nor me. Our reputations…they are my concern…we won't survive…

Pause.

RICH: If I may ask…are you –

ISABELLA: – I hear you are commissioning a libretto. For a new opera. How exciting.

RICH: I am trying to, but finding these singers…

ISABELLA: Theatres need surprises. Celebrity.

RICH: Thin on the ground.

ISABELLA: So many young and talented producers nowadays, Mr Rich. The world does not recognize maturity

RICH is very quiet.

RICH: He won't return. He left.

ISABELLA: Well, this is how I'll do it. I will tell him…that, now the King is gone, I have no further use for him. That his contract with us is now at an end.

Write to him. I will let you know when he is on his way to London.

RICH: Majesty. I will do everything I can.

ISABELLA: It really is so beautiful here. More real than life. *(Beat.)* I hope your world will be…kind to him. *(She offers her hand. He kisses it. She looks out again at the auditorium.)* Farinelli…he will be known when we are long extinguished. Time will record us as echoes only; distant stars; tricks of the light. *(She leaves.)* Goodbye Mr. Rich.

She is gone. The curtain rises, revealing FARINELLI in the attic of his house in Bologna. We have jumped forwards a little in time – a few months. He is reading a letter: in an alcove of the empty room – save for one chair – are piled precious objects: instruments, paintings, and the like.

(FARINELLI is revealed upstage.)

RICH: Time. It's a strange thing. It curls one way then takes you round the other way so you meet yourself coming home. It's been twenty-two years. A half life. What will we say to one another? Can he still sing like he did? If he can…

My dear Farinelli, I hope this letter finds you…

SCENE 7. CONTINUOUS.

FARINELLI: How did he find me?

RICH: Finally I've tracked you down. I heard about your… change of circumstances. Better out of Spain, but what the hell are you doing in Bologna of all places?

FARINELLI: He writes about the weather in London –

RICH: It's raining. The price of oysters has *soared.*

FARINELLI: Oh, he says 'I met your Dr Cervi by chance at The Royal Society: apparently they like his nonsense and have made him a Fellow.'

RICH: People will believe anything, it seems… Even that the stars above us make a nice noise.

FARINELLI: A nice noise. Oh… There's a new opera!

RICH: Now it is ready. And the part that's written for you – oh what a part – you have never sung anything like this before. It will take every bit of your heart, your soul, your spirit, it will take all you have, but is written for you to sing, and you alone.

FARINELLI: Written for me alone. Me alone.

RICH: We are all very tired of that imposter Tenducci groaning through your best arias. Your audience is longing for your return.

FARINELLI: My return.

RICH: You should see our new theatre! Your voice will sound magnificent. London will be at your feet. It will be like old times. But better. Much, much better… I promise…

FARINELLI: You promise.

There is a knock on the door downstairs.

FARINELLI: *(Calls.)* Come in. The door is open.

TAILOR: Maestro Farinelli. I am sorry if I disturb you.

FARINELLI: Vincenzo! What a surprise! Do come up. I'm in the attic. Oh – have you brought my new coat with you?

TAILOR: Yes Maestro. I was thinking that you will be needing it; the weather is turning.

FARINELLI: How thoughtful. You feel the seasons here; it would still be warm in Madrid…have a seat. Would you like something to drink? A little rum?

TAILOR: It is the middle of the morning, Maestro.

FARINELLI: Even better. Tonic for the blood. *(He pours a glass of rum for the TAILOR.)*

TAILOR: It's a very humble house you have. But up here – full of wonderful things.

FARINELLI: Presents. I keep them for others. People who come by. Look at this. A little bird in a cage. These are real jewels in the bird's eyes. And he sings! Listen! *(He winds up the key in the side of the cage. The bird sings for a little then stops in mid-song.)* Isn't it charming! I was given it during my time in Spain.

TAILOR: It is extraordinary. Very pretty.

FARINELLI: Take it would you? As payment…or part payment for the coat.

TAILOR: No, I could not.

FARINELLI: Please. It would give me pleasure.

TAILOR: I do not want to hear a mechanical bird singing.

FARINELLI: You need never wind it up, then! Just the jewels alone –

TAILOR: I want to hear you sing.

FARINELLI: That is an impossible bargain. I do not sing.

TAILOR: I think you do.

FARINELLI: Then I will not. I haven't sung to anyone in years. My voice –

TAILOR: – I have heard that your voice cured a King from madness.

FARINELLI: No. It kept away the other voices, that's all.

TAILOR: So he was filled with music and had no room for sorrow.

FARINELLI: His madness was a kind of sorrow, now you say so.

TAILOR: A humble tailor understands sorrow as well as a King.

FARINELLI: Please don't ask me, Vincenzo.

TAILOR: Then you do not wish to have your coat, then, and my labour will be in vain, and I shall have to go away and take the coat away with me, and try to sell it on to someone for whom it was not made and is a bad fit. This you would do to me.

FARINELLI: You strike a hard bargain.

Pause.

TAILOR: It is a beautiful coat. Such cloth. Feel it, how soft and warm it is.

FARINELLI: What would you have me sing? A love-song or a song of good life?

TAILOR: Neither. 'Lascia ch'io pianga'.

FARINELLI: 'Lascia'? Why that one?

TAILOR: I heard you sing it once. In Naples, in that big opera house. It means 'Let me weep'. I wept. I was only a small boy. About ten years old.

FARINELLI: Ten years old you say. That's too old, and also too young.

He sings. The TAILOR holds the coat close to his chest. FARINELLI sings 'Lascia ch'io pianga' (in full) from 'Rinaldo' by Handel. The voice is as splendid as it always was, always has been. FARINELLI looks again at the letter he is holding.

During the song (the instrumental part of the song, over the music), the TAILOR asks:

TAILOR: You sang this to the King. Yes?

FARINELLI: Yes. Nobody else wanted it.

TAILOR: Was it his favourite?

FARINELLI: It was the only song in the end.

TAILOR: I understand.

The song continues… The sung part finishes… Under the last bars of the instrumental music, the SINGER places his hand on FARINELLI's shoulder…the two look at each other…'CARLO' and 'FARINELLI' connect and…make their peace with each other; FARINELLI exits, CARLO tears up the letter. He is at peace.

THE END.